Garden Therapy

Garden Therapy

written by
Ted O'Neal

illustrated by
R.W. Alley

ONE
CARING
PLACE

Abbey Press

Text © 1999 by Ted O'Neal
Illustrations © 1999 by St. Meinrad Archabbey
Published by One Caring Place
Abbey Press
St. Meinrad, Indiana 47577

Library of Congress Catalog Number
98-74886

ISBN 0-87029-325-7

Printed in the United States of America

Foreword

"We've got to get ourselves back to the garden."
So went the line from a popular song in the 1960s.
And while part of the reference was to the Garden of
Eden, the message was also about "getting back" to
the basics, the simple, the good…back to nature
and our connecting with it.

For wanna-be, would-be, or veteran gardeners—
or those who simply appreciate the sight and scent
of a garden—this handy little guide honors the
natural, nurturing experience of going to the garden.
Garden Therapy especially celebrates the popular
"connecting-with-nature" experience we call "gardening." Even more, this book celebrates the healing
power of sowing, waiting, weeding, tending, reaping,
and savoring.

Gardens teach, gardens comfort, gardens make
us grow! After all, each of us is given a land to toil, a
garden to tend, be it large or small or in-between.
Take care of it—and the whole world turns…bright.

1.

Experiencing nature through gardening satisfies our spirit and our emotions like nothing else. Raise your spirits while you're raising those flowers and fruits and vegetables.

2.

Gardens show us the miracle not only of birth—but of rebirth. With nature we enter into decay and decline—and death itself—but we come back rejoicing. Garden...and grow in faith.

3.

Gardening teaches us the value of planning, preparation, taking care, nurturing. Make some plans and ready the soil.

4.

When we work the soil, we commingle with the very substance of our being and sustenance. Dig it!

5.

With nature we take a leap
of faith, trusting that the
small seed we sow will sprout
and grow and flourish. Let
nature's miracle speak to your
faith in God, in creation, and
in yourself.

6.

Sometimes it's better to just plant a garden for the planting of it rather than for the harvest it may yield. Let the planting itself be your harvest!

7.

Planting a garden shows your faith in tomorrow, and tending a garden shows your investment in tomorrow and today. Invest in, and believe in, tomorrow and today.

8.

As partakers in creation, we bring seed and nutrient, care and feeding, water and weeding to our garden. But God brings the growth. Give God credit.

9.

Even if you live at the top of a skyscraper, you can grow a garden and be in deep-down touch with creation. Set your pot in the window.

10.

Gardening helps us get our minds off our own growing concerns and onto a real growing concern. Get something good growing.

11.

God also planted a garden in your imagination. You can create a wildflower meadow in your mind no matter where you are.

12.

Caring gardeners are vigilant gardeners. There are usually warning signs when weeds, frost, insects, drought, or storm are a threat. Learn the art of "being prepared," and the same good habit can work wonders in other parts of your life.

13.

Gardeners know that even better things than money grow on trees. And you can practically live on the interest. Invest!

14.

By caring for plants we become
caregivers. As we become good
stewards of our little corners
of the world, we grow in
confidence in our abilities.
Take pride in that.

15.

In the garden, we learn to take the good with the bad. But sometimes we have to face the fact that it's time to pull up some weeds. Take pleasure in the improvement you make.

16.

Gardens and nature teach us the necessity of waiting and the virtue of patience. Accept the fact that through much of life we live in incompleteness and on-the-way-ness. We're still growing.

17.

Gardens and nature invite us in to weed and tend, but also to enjoy some quiet rest and solitude. Accept the invitation; pause in the silence; let your soul be soothed.

18.

If we're under God's heaven,
we're in God's garden. Enjoy it,
come field or forest, rain or
shine! We are by nature blessed.

19.

We are all planted in a time
and in a place. Revere the
sacredness of your time in
your particular garden.

20.

Nature and gardening let us co-create and re-create—with joy. Could it be that God created <u>us</u> for the simple enjoyment of doing so?!

21.

Garden space is sacred space. Let the produce from your garden feed your body—and your soul with holiness and wholeness.

22.

Gardening and working with nature can be in themselves forms of prayer. When we "con-template" nature in our garden, we make a "temple" upon the sacred ground we toil. Worship today in the temple of your choice!

23.

We don't need a lot of land or money to garden or to enjoy nature. Get yourself caught up in the "free gift" of some of the best things in life.

24.

Searching for the season's first blossom is a blessing in itself. Even if it's too early, you will awaken your own spirit hiding under the snow and ice.

25.

Gardening teaches us about the interrelationships and interdependence of all creation. We are part of it all. Enjoy the company!

26.

Gardening and nature prove that we are not really in control: God is. But God is counting on us to help make something beautiful in the garden of our lives.

27.

Gardening and nature remind us we are a part of something much bigger than we can possibly comprehend: something that preceded us and will succeed us. Let this insight help you keep life's challenges in their proper perspective.

28.

A garden connects us to the world in more ways than we know. Take up the challenge of finding out more and more about gardening and nature— and finding out more and more about life and yourself!

29.

We are all given a land to toil, a garden to tend, be it large or small or in-between. Take care of it—and the whole world turns...bright.

30.

We are always trying to
re-create the paradise we once
shared in the garden with God.
Getting back to that garden
may be easier than we think.
Part of it may be right there
at the tip of your green thumb.

31.

Flowers and plants are love letters from the earth. Enjoy and savor them like great poetry.

32.

Behind that patch of beautiful garden flowers you may just find a sweaty, bug-bitten, dirt-covered, thorn-torn gardener. Notice the satisfied smile. It's telling you something.

33.

We may be going "from ashes to ashes and dust to dust," but there are some incredible natural delights along the way. Go ahead and get some dirt under those fingernails.

34.

The best gardens show a lot of variety. And, don't forget, you can define "weed" any way you like!

35.

The real beauty of many a garden is its untended, "natural" look. Sometimes we can improve our world by simply leaving things alone.

36.

We are all of "the garden variety"—ordinarily extraordinary! Bloom away!

ELF HOLLOW GARDEN FAIR

AWARDS

PRIZES

37.

The fruits of our fields are many—beyond the food for our tables. Take delight in the feasts nature gives our senses and souls.

38.

After a while, you come to the wonderful realization that you're not only taking care of the garden—the garden is taking care of you. Take care!

Ted O'Neal is a writer, gardener, father, husband, and dog-walker who lives in Southern Indiana.

Illustrator for the Abbey Press Elf-help Books, **R.W. Alley** also illustrates and writes children's books. He lives in Barrington, Rhode Island, with his wife, daughter, and son.

The Story of the Abbey Press Elves

The engaging figures that populate the Abbey Press "elf-help" line of publications and products first appeared in 1987 on the pages of a small self-help book called *Be-good-to-yourself Therapy*. Shaped by the publishing staff's vision and defined in R.W. Alley's inventive illustrations, they lived out author Cherry Hartman's gentle, self-nurturing advice with charm, poignancy, and humor.

Reader response was so enthusiastic that more Elf-help Books were soon under way, a still-growing series that has inspired a line of related gift products.

The especially endearing character featured in the early books—sporting a cap with a mood-changing candle in its peak—has since been joined by a spirited female elf with flowers in her hair.

These two exuberant, sensitive, resourceful, kindhearted, lovable sprites, along with their lively elfin community, reveal what's truly important as they offer messages of joy and wonder, playfulness and co-creation, wholeness and serenity, the miracle of life and the mystery of God's love.

With wisdom and whimsy, these little creatures with long noses demonstrate the elf-help way to a rich and fulfilling life.

Elf-help Books

...adding "a little character" and a lot
of help to self-help reading!

Garden Therapy

#20116 $4.95   ISBN 0-87029-325-7

Elf-help for Busy Moms

#20117 $4.95   ISBN 0-87029-324-9

Trust-in-God Therapy

#20119 $4.95   ISBN 0-87029-322-2

Elf-help for Overcoming Depression

#20134 $4.95   ISBN 0-87029-315-X

New Baby Therapy

#20140 $4.95   ISBN 0-87029-307-9

Grief Therapy for Men

#20141 $4.95   ISBN 0-87029-306-0

Living From Your Soul

#20146 $4.95   ISBN 0-87029-303-6

Teacher Therapy

#20145 $4.95   ISBN 0-87029-302-8

Be-good-to-your-family Therapy

#20154 $4.95   ISBN 0-87029-300-1

Stress Therapy

#20153 $4.95   ISBN 0-87029-301-X

Making-sense-out-of-suffering Therapy

#20156 $4.95   ISBN 0-87029-296-X

Get Well Therapy

#20157 $4.95   ISBN 0-87029-297-8